TUDOR
1485-1603

STUART
1603-1714

GEORGIAN
1714-1837

VICTORIAN
1837-1901

MODERN TIMES
1902-NOW

# children's HISTORY of SUNDERLAND

Written by
Keith Gregson

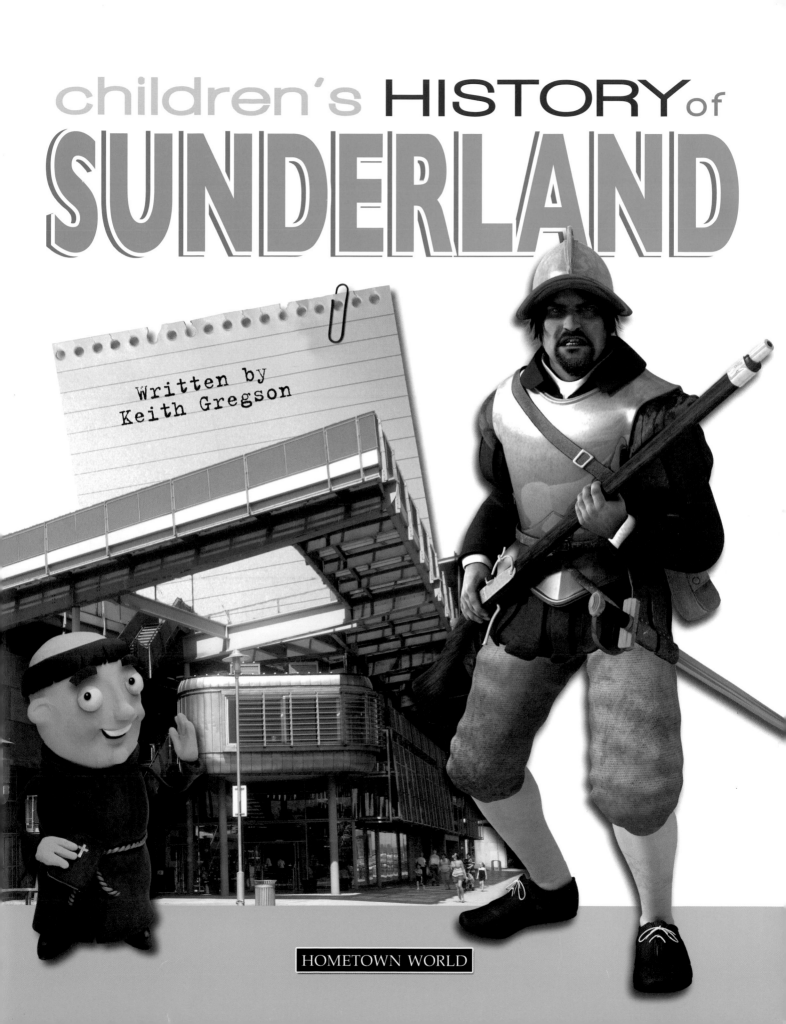

HOMETOWN WORLD

# How well do you know your city?

Have you ever wondered what it would have been like living in Sunderland when the Romans arrived? What about working in the coal mine instead of going to school? This book will uncover the important and exciting things that happened in your city.

Want to hear the other good bits? You will love this book! Some rather brainy folk have worked on it to make sure it's fun and informative. So what are you waiting for? Peel back the pages and be amazed at your city's very own story.

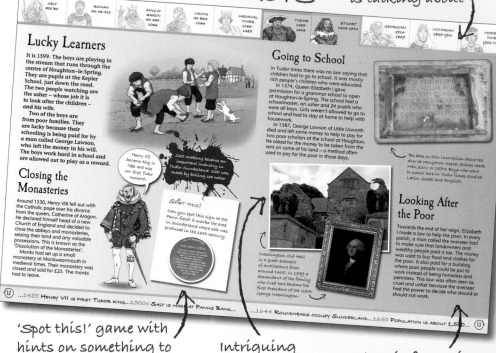

Timeline shows which period (dates and people) each spread is talking about

'Spot this!' game with hints on something to find in your city

Intriguing photos

Clear informative text

Fun facts to amaze you!

Go back in time to read what it was like for children growing up in Sunderland.

Each period in the book ends with a summary explaining how we know about the past.

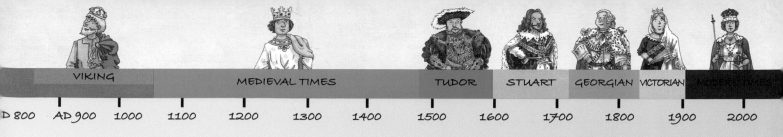

# Contents

CELT
500 BC

ROMAN
AD 43-410

ANGLO-SAXON
AD 450-1066

VIKING
AD 865-1066

MEDIEVAL TIMES
1066-1485

# Stopped by a Soldier

Ardal is worried because the Roman soldier has stopped him. Ardal explains that he was just picking up some wood for the fire when he strayed close to the watchtower.

The Romans have been there for years now, watching over the little supply boats as they travel up and down the river. Some soldiers have been putting big stones in the river further upstream to make it deeper and allow bigger supply boats to travel nearer to the fort on the road.

The soldier puts up his sword and smiles. "Off you go," he says. "Watch where you are walking next time!"

# Supplying the Soldiers

The Romans came to Britain to settle in AD 43. Within 100 years they had built forts, towns, roads and a huge wall from coast to coast just north of Sunderland. This wall was built for the Emperor Hadrian and became known as Hadrian's Wall. It was a kind of frontier and had lots of forts spaced along it. The Romans took food and supplies to these forts either by road or by sea and river.

The main road from the south to Hadrian's Wall went through Chester-le-Street, 16 kilometres inland from Sunderland on the River Wear. The main river route was on the River Tyne with its supply port at South Shields. The Romans might have used the River Wear to supply the fort at Chester-le-Street. There may have been a small Roman fort or watchtower where Sunderland is today, and a dam near Hylton, where there is now a big bridge over the A19 road.

My countrymen named a wall after me. Can you guess who I am?

SPOT THIS!

This bridge at Hylton was built in the 20th century. But what might have been below it almost 2,000 years ago?

AD 43 ROMANS ARRIVE IN BRITAIN...AD 122 HADRIAN'S WALL IS BEGUN...

TUDOR
1485-1603

STUART
1603-1714

GEORGIAN
1714-1837

VICTORIAN
1837-1901

MODERN
TIMES
1902-NOW

A typical
Roman fort

Roman coins show us
the emperor who was
ruling at the time.
This helps historians to
work out dates.

## How do we know?

We know very little about Roman Sunderland,
but there is evidence that the Britons were
around here when the Romans came. A bronze
statue was discovered in a quarry and a log
boat made by Britons was found in the river.
The log boat may even date back to pre-Roman
times. We also have Roman coins and pots.

The remains of Roman roads have been found
in Sunderland and there is a possibility
that a recorded fort may have been here,
although no evidence of this has yet been
found in the ground. Up until the 19th
century there were large stones in the
river between North Hylton and South Hylton.
Some people think the stones were part of a
bridge or causeway, but others think it was
a kind of dam or weir built by the Romans
to make the water deeper between Hylton and
Chester-le-Street.

The Romans didn't
settle in Sunderland
but they might have
had a signal tower
here.

...AROUND AD 129 ROMAN LEGIONS FINISH WORK ON HADRIAN'S WALL...

5

# To School by Boat

The sun comes from behind a cloud on a warm summer's day. It is AD 682 and eight-year-old Edwin is being rowed across the River Wear by his father in a small rowing boat. Despite the sun's warmth, Edwin shivers with excitement. Ahead of him lies the monastery of St Peter at Monkwearmouth where his neighbour Baeda was sent a couple of years ago to learn to read and write.

Edwin's father asked if his son could go there too and Edwin has been accepted. Maybe he will become a monk. Or perhaps he will learn to illustrate the fine books that are made at the monastery. Exciting times lie ahead!

# Saxon Times

After the Romans left, England was unprotected and open to new invaders who came from Denmark and northern Germany to settle in England. They became known as Anglo-Saxons. Most of these people were farmers who lived in small villages with wooden huts surrounded by wooden fences and a ditch to keep out animals and invaders. The chief or 'thane' would have lived in a big hall.

The area now covered by the City of Sunderland would have been open land with a scattering of huts or small villages. When the monastery was built in AD 674, the appearance of a large stone building would probably have been quite a surprise to local people.

During Saxon times, the Sunderland area was part of Northumbria – a large and important kingdom.

Map of Saxon Kingdoms AD 600–900

PICTLAND

STRATHCLYDE

Hadrian's Wall

NORTHUMBRIA

LINDSEY

EAST ANGLIA

MERCIA

ESSEX

HWICCA

WESSEX

KENT

SUSSEX

...AD 673 BEDE IS BORN AT WEARMOUTH...AD 674 ST PETER'S IS FOUNDED...

# The Church

The Anglo-Saxons brought Christianity to England. By the time Edwin went to St Peter's, monasteries and churches could be seen all over the land.

Monks lived in monasteries and led a simple life. They produced their own food and made their own clothes, spending most of their time in prayer and study. One of their greatest skills lay in making fine books, especially bibles. The monks wrote and illustrated these bibles by hand. One of the bibles partly made at St Peter's is now in a library in Florence, Italy. It is called the Codex Amiantinus and is one of the most precious books in the world.

Edwin was being rowed to the monastery that is now St Peter's Church.

### Sᴘᴏᴛ ᴛʜɪꜱ!

St Peter's Church has changed over time but parts of it are from Saxon times, such as the tower and the west wall.

Most people in Saxon times would have lived in huts like this one.

## Benedict Biscop

Bede's teacher was a man called Benedict Biscop. Biscop built St Peter's and, a few years later, St Paul's monastery at Jarrow on the River Tyne. The monasteries were close enough for the monks to walk between them. Bede called them 'one monastery in two places'.

Biscop was a great tourist. He went to Rome six times in his life in an age when transport was difficult. He also followed the Roman idea of building in stone and introduced coloured glass into the windows of his monasteries.

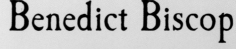

Benedict Biscop is the patron saint of the City of Sunderland.

## Bede

Edwin's friend Baeda is known nowadays as Bede. He went to St Peter's when he was only seven years old. Later Bede wrote the first history of the English people in Latin and also translated some of the bible.

If Edwin had kept a journal he might have written something similar to the account on the right. It is now July AD 716. By this time Edwin would have been at the monastery for 34 years.

You need a lot of patience and a steady hand for this job.

It seems such a long time since my father rowed me across the river to St Peter's and I'm still here. I'm much older now – but I am happy.

Just last week, the abbot of St Paul's set off for Rome with the bible we have been working on for years. I helped with the illustrations. It will be a long journey over land and sea.

My friend Baeda never stops writing. He is living at St Paul's now and has worked out a calendar for fixing when Easter should happen each year. He also says we should date our years from when Jesus was born. This is called Anno Domini which means 'the Year of Our Lord'.

Our teacher, Benedict, died when I was still young. We buried him near to the altar. The others are working in the fields but I am allowed to stay in because of my age. It is time for the last service of the day in the church so I must finish writing now.

+ CENOBIUM AD EXIMII MERITO
UENERABILES AL UXTORIS
quem CAPUT ECCLESIAE
DEDICAT ALTA FIDES
PETRUS LANGOBARDORUM
EXTREMIS DEFINIB· ABBAS
DEUOTI AFFECTUS
PIGNORA MITTO MEI
MEQUE MEOSQ·OPTANS
TANTI INTER GAUDIA PATRIS
IN CAELIS MEMOREM
SEMPER HABERE LOCUM

This is a page from the Codex Amiantinus – the bible that Bede worked on at St Peter's and St Paul's.

An illustration from the Codex Amiantinus

TUDOR
1485-1603

STUART
1603-1714

GEORGIAN
1714-1837

VICTORIAN
1837-1901

MODERN
TIMES
1902-NOW

Illustrated
script in
a modern
sculpture
→

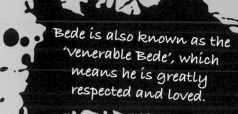

Bede is also known as the 'Venerable Bede', which means he is greatly respected and loved.

Most people who lived here in Saxon times were monks, farmers or fishermen.

# How do we know?

Apart from the Saxon parts of St Peter's Church, there is very little evidence of the Saxons in our area. This is partly because the Saxons built their homes from wood, which rots easily.

St Paul's Church at Jarrow is now part of a big visitors' centre called 'Bede's World' where you can see how Saxon monks used to live. Archaeologists have also found pieces of the coloured glass used in the windows of the monasteries. Some of this precious stained glass can be seen in Sunderland Museum and Winter Gardens.

Bede wrote several books that tell us exactly what happened here in Saxon times. His best-known book is 'A History of the English People'. Copies of this book have been sold for 1,300 years! One of Bede's greatest stories is about Benedict Biscop and how he managed to bring one of the greatest musicians of the time back with him from Rome. The musician's name was John and he took charge of the choir at St Peter's. Bede said that people came from all over Britain to learn about music from John.

CELT
500 BC

ROMAN
AD 43-410

ANGLO-
SAXON
AD 450-
1066

VIKING
AD 865-
1066

MEDIEVA
TIMES
1066-148

# Home from Work

It is 1396 and it has been a long day for Gilbert. He has had a slow journey by boat and road all the way from Whitby, where he delivered coal to the monks at Whitby Abbey. The monks paid him in cash but also gave him some food and drink that is now getting wet in the heavy rain.

Gilbert works with his brother to find and sell coal. They use a ship built on the River Wear to transport their coal. Gilbert is looking forward to seeing his brother and hopes he has found more coal for them to sell. But right now Gilbert can't wait to get home.

# A Fishing Village

Almost 700 years passed between Saxon times and the arrival of the first Tudor monarch. It is likely that the Vikings, who came from Scandinavia, attacked St Peter's monastery at some point and destroyed most of it.

After this, a small fishing village started to grow and a church was built for the people living in the Bishopwearmouth area – where the city centre is today. By the 14th century, wooden ships were being built on the River Wear and coal was being mined not far from the river.

Miners worked in bell pits where men and coal buckets were hauled up and down on the end of a rope. Bell pits were not very big. The miners didn't want to tunnel too far underground in case the roof of the pit collapsed. This was a small start but coal mining and shipbuilding were to become two very important Sunderland industries in the future.

*A cross-section of a medieval bell pit*

SPOT THIS!
Hylton Castle is believed to have a ghost – the Cauld Lad of Hylton. Can you find out how the poor boy died?

The Houghton Feast takes place in Houghton-le-Spring every October and dates back to the 12th century.

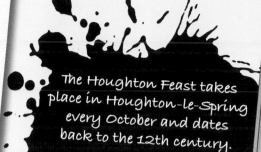

The tradition of the Houghton Feast was revived in 1967, when this photo was probably taken.

Sunderland was a small fishing village in medieval times.

## How do we know?

The Vikings raided the north east and destroyed Holy Island. Archaeologists think that the same Vikings may have attacked St Peter's or that the monks left the monastery in fear.

One document from the 14th century says that a man called Thomas Menville was given the right to build ships at Hendon in 1346. Another document says that coal was being taken down the River Wear in 1396 and carried to the monks in Whitby Abbey.

We also know that there was a castle or fortified manor house at Hylton at this time. Stones in Hylton Castle and Hylton Castle Chapel show that building was going on around the year 1400. Parts of St Michael's Church at Bishopwearmouth – now Sunderland Minster – were also built in medieval times.

# Lucky Learners

It is 1599. The boys are playing in the stream that runs through the centre of Houghton-le-Spring. They are pupils at the Kepier School, just down the road. The two people watching are the usher – whose job it is to look after the children – and his wife.

Two of the boys are from poor families. They are lucky because their schooling is being paid for by a man called George Lawson, who left the money in his will. The boys work hard in school and are allowed out to play as a reward.

Henry VII became king in 1485 and was our first Tudor monarch.

Salt-making became an important industry in Tudor Sunderland. Salt was made by boiling sea water.

## SPOT THIS!

Can you spot this sign at Panns Bank? It marks the area in Sunderland where salt was produced in the 16th century.

### City of Sunderland
### THE PANN FIELD

This area became known as The Panns in the 16th century when it was the centre of the salt industry. Sea water was boiled in huge pans 20ft or more across and 6ft deep; a furnace below repeatedly boiled the pans dry for 3 days to produce salt.

# Closing the Monasteries

Around 1530, Henry VIII fell out with the Catholic pope over his divorce from the queen, Catherine of Aragon. He declared himself head of a new Church of England and decided to close the abbeys and monasteries, seizing their land and any valuable possessions. This is known as the 'Dissolution of the Monasteries'.

Monks had set up a small monastery at Monkwearmouth in medieval times. Their monastery was closed and sold for £25. The monks had to leave.

# Going to School

In Tudor times there was no law saying that children had to go to school. It was mostly rich people's children who were educated.

In 1574, Queen Elizabeth I gave permission for a grammar school to open at Houghton-le-Spring. The school had a schoolmaster, an usher and 24 pupils who were all boys. Girls weren't allowed to go to school and had to stay at home to help with housework.

In 1587, George Lawson of Little Usworth died and left some money to help to pay for two poor scholars at the school at Houghton. He asked for the money to be taken from the rent on some of his land – a method often used to pay for the poor in those days.

The date in this inscription above the door at Houghton Kepier School reads MDLXXIV (or 1574). Boys who went to school here in Tudor times studied Latin, Greek and English.

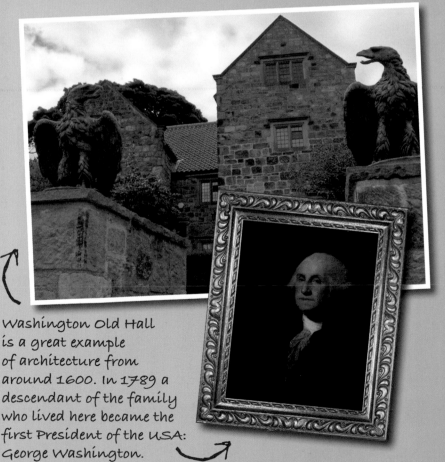

Washington Old Hall is a great example of architecture from around 1600. In 1789 a descendant of the family who lived here became the first President of the USA: George Washington.

# Looking After the Poor

Towards the end of her reign, Elizabeth I made a law to help the poor. In every parish, a man called the overseer had to make sure that landowners and wealthy people paid a tax. The money was used to buy food and clothes for the poor. It also paid for a building where poor people could be put to work instead of being homeless and penniless. This law was often seen as cruel and unfair because the overseer had the power to decide who should or should not work.

...1574 HOUGHTON GRAMMAR SCHOOL IS BUILT...1587 LAWSON HELPS SCHOLARS...

13

CELT
500 BC

ROMAN
AD 43-410

ANGLO-
SAXON
AD 450-
1066

VIKING
AD 865-
1066

MEDIEVA
TIMES
1066-
1485

# Bernard Gilpin

Bernard Gilpin was the rector of Houghton-le-Spring in the late 16th century. Bernard believed that kings and queens should have more say in organizing their churches than the pope in Rome and that ordinary people should be able to make up their own minds about God by reading the Bible.

Queen Mary I wanted to keep the old ways and to return to the Catholic faith with the pope as leader of all Christians. She became so angry with Bernard that she ordered him to London, probably to have him executed or burned at the stake. But on the way to London, he fell off his horse and broke his leg. While Bernard was getting better, Mary died. The new queen, Elizabeth I, did not have the same beliefs as Mary, so Bernard was able to return to Houghton to live and work. He died in 1583.

In the imagined account below, a young girl called Anne is writing to her mother in 1558. Anne and her father have just witnessed Bernard Gilpin's return to Houghton.

If the rector hadn't fallen off his horse, he might have been executed by Queen Mary!

You should have been there, Mother! By the time we reached the church gates there was a big crowd and everybody was cheering. A messenger had just told us that the rector was only a few minutes away. Father says that the rector is a very lucky man and that we have the new queen to thank for sending him back to us in one piece.

An even bigger cheer went up as the rector appeared on his horse, surrounded by friends. One of his friends quickly got down to help him dismount. The rector was limping badly. He stood at the gate and asked for three cheers for the new queen and the new religion.

Father said he wished he could be a guest at the big house tonight. There was going to be a huge feast and even the horses would have a good time! We must all go to church on Sunday to hear what the rector has to say about the new religion.

Queen Elizabeth I ensured Bernard's safe return to Houghton.

The Bernard Gilpin Primary School is named after this famous Sunderland rector.

Bernard Gilpin was like a local celebrity in Tudor times!

By 1650, the population in Sunderland had grown to about 1,500.

## How do we know?

People have written biographies of Bernard Gilpin since Tudor times. When he came to Houghton, Gilpin told local people about his religious ideas. He was known for his community feasts and he looked after many famous visitors. People said at the time that if a horse became lost, it would head for Bernard Gilpin's stables because the horse knew it would be well looked after there!

With the permission of Elizabeth I, Bernard was also able to help set up the Kepier School. The school was at Kepier Hall, which is still used today as a community centre.

Meanwhile, at Washington Old Hall the rooms are laid out as they would have been in Tudor and Stuart times.

# The Bridge Opens

George has found himself a good spot on top of the riverbank. He is pleased that he is able to see over the top of the huge crowd, as he is not very tall. What a day it is for folks on both sides of the river! At last a bridge is going to join Monkwearmouth in the north and Bishopwearmouth in the south. There will be no more waiting for a ferry and no need to take the long journey up to the nearest river crossing.

There is a great roar as the bridge is declared open and the crowds pour onto it. George watches with pride.

# Civil War

The River Wear became even more important after the Wearmouth Bridge was built. But before this, the banks of the river were also useful during the Civil War.

Civil War broke out in England in 1642. Royalists, who supported King Charles I, fought the Roundheads who supported Parliament. Small battles took place near Sunderland, where most people supported Parliament. From 1644 to 1647 Sunderland was the base for a Scottish army who fought as allies of the English Parliament. This army set up a camp beside the River Wear.

When Parliament eventually won the war it was not happy that coal was being carried along the River Tyne in Newcastle because Newcastle had supported the king. It decided that the River Wear should be used for transporting coal instead. This was a great boost for Sunderland. The town grew quickly after this and by 1796 the decision was made to build a bridge across the River Wear.

We were nicknamed the Roundheads because of our short hairstyles!

Royalists were also known as Cavaliers. They supported the king, Charles I.

# Hero of Camperdown

In 1797 the British navy fought the Dutch at the Battle of Camperdown. During the battle, the mast on Britain's HMS *Venerable* was hit and the admiral's flag fell down. This was an accidental sign of surrender so Sunderland sailor, Jack Crawford, climbed the mast to nail the flag back in place. He was fired at the whole time. After winning the battle, HMS *Venerable* returned home and Crawford became known as the 'Hero of Camperdown'. The people of Sunderland presented him with a silver medal for his bravery.

SP☊T THIS!

There is a statue in memory of Sunderland hero Jack Crawford in Mowbray Park. Can you find it?

Sunderland City Council

**WEARMOUTH BRIDGE**
The first Wearmouth Bridge of 1796 proved to be a catalyst for the growth of Sunderland. It was rebuilt in 1857 by Robert Stephenson and again in 1927 when this steel arch bridge was constructed to a design by Mott, Hay and Anderson.

This plaque marks the first Wearmouth Bridge.

Sunderland grew very quickly during the later years of Georgian times.

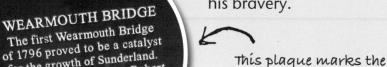

## How do we know?

A great deal has been written about the Civil War by people who were there at the time and by historians since. A blue plaque on the car park just south of the Wearmouth Bridge marks the spot where the Scottish army camped. A cannon was also found in the river nearby.

We also have an excellent record of the opening of the bridge as, by 1796, Sunderland was becoming famous for its special pottery. Pots were made to celebrate people and events. The Museum and Winter Gardens has a collection of pots decorated with pictures of the bridge opening, as well as pots remembering the bravery of local sailor, Jack Crawford.

# Off to the Mine

It's five o'clock in the morning and winter. It is cold and dark. Ten-year-old Alexander shivers as he gets out of bed and puts on his work clothes. His mum gives him a pot of coffee and some food, known as bait. Then he trudges up the road to meet his friend, Nicholas.

The boys work as trappers in the coal mine beside the river. Their job is to open and close the trap doors in the narrow underground corridors to let the trucks through and to stop any gas building up. The boys will both be there until night-time. Nicholas is scared of the dark but he doesn't dare light a candle in case it catches some gas and causes an explosion.

Mining was the main industry in Sunderland at this time.

SPOT THIS!
There are special open days at Washington 'F' Pit where you can see a working engine house.

# Coal Mining Grows

In the 19th and 20th centuries there were many coal mines in the area now covered by the City of Sunderland. There were mines, for example, at Ryhope, Hetton-le-Hole, Hylton, Silksworth, Houghton-le-Spring, Washington and Herrington. These mines were much more advanced than bell pits and had metal cages that transported miners, supplies and coal to and from the pit.

Before the 1840s, in particular, coal mining could be very dangerous especially for young boys and girls who looked after the trap doors and carried the coal to the cages.

...1812 EXPLOSION AT FELLING PIT...1813 CLANNY LAMP IS INVENTED...

# Fight for Safety

In the early 19th century more and more coal was needed to run factories and machinery. Miners had to work quickly and safely. In 1812 an explosion at Felling Pit in Gateshead killed 92 people, including several young boys. Engineers started designing safety lamps that would allow the miners to see while they were working and which would warn them if gas was building up.

Dr William Clanny was an Irishman living in Sunderland. In 1813 he invented a safety lamp that became known as the Clanny Lamp. On Tyneside, George Stephenson – who went on to become a famous railway engineer – developed the Geordie Lamp. Meanwhile the Davy Lamp was named after its inventor, Humphry Davy in Cornwall.

Have you heard about these new Granny lamps?

I think you mean Clanny lamps.

You can see a Clanny Lamp at Sunderland Museum.

The Stadium of Light was built on the site of the old Monkwearmouth Colliery.

Here's Dr William Clanny, proudly holding his great invention.

# Cages and Pumps

The safety lamp was not the only invention to make life easier and safer for people working in mines. In the early days, miners used ladders to get up and down or they jumped into the baskets used for carrying coal. The rope used for hauling the basket often snapped causing injury and death. In later years, cages replaced the baskets and steel ropes were used.

Water underground was also a problem until mine owners started to use pumps developed by Thomas Newcomen and James Watt. Soon steam engines were being used to haul the cages up and down and to drive the pumps which removed the water. Most pits had pit heaps for the waste from the mine and a pit pond for the water. Some of these ponds were used as swimming pools!

In 1842 the government decided to find out what life was like for people working in mines. It sent inspectors around the country to talk to the workers.

The account on the right shows an imaginary discussion between an inspector and a young mine worker called Mary Harrison. This interview takes place at Wearside coal mine on 3rd March, 1842.

There is a lot of sulphur in the pit. It stinks of rotten eggs!

**Mr Young:** "How old were you when you first came to the mine?"

**Mary:** "I was six years old, sir."

**Mr Young:** "And what was your work then?"

**Mary:** "I used to sort the stone out from the coal."

**Mr Young:** "How old are you now?"

**Mary:** "I was ten last birthday."

**Mr Young:** "Do you still sort stone out?"

**Mary:** "No, sir. I work underground, taking the coal from where the men dig to the carts."

**Mr Young:** "Do you find the work hard?"

**Mary:** "Very. I have to drag a big basket full of coal down the tunnel. The best way is by joining a chain to my belt and then to the basket. The chain goes between my legs and it really hurts."

**Mr Young:** "And what is it like underground?"

**Mary:** "It is very hot and very smelly. Sometimes I feel sick and I cannot eat the food my mother has given me as bait."

Mark Swaddle was a mine engine driver from Washington. He kept a diary from 1867 to 1917. This is a page from his diary.

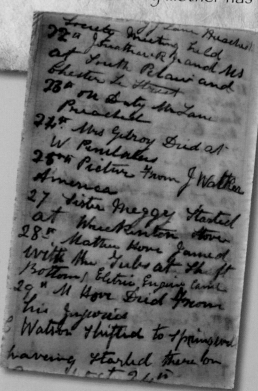

UDOR 1485-1603

STUART 1603-1714

GEORGIAN 1714-1837

VICTORIAN 1837-1901

MODERN TIMES
1902-NOW

Many Victorian women worked as housekeepers or maids. This document shows how much they could expect to earn in a year in old pounds and shillings.

Many of the big houses in Roker and Ashbrooke had three or four servants.

| Class of work | Age | Average yearly wage |
|---|---|---|
| Between maid | 19 | £10 7s |
| Scullery maid | 19 | £13 |
| Kitchen maid | 20 | £15 |
| Nurse-housemaid | 21-25 | £16 |
| General domestic | 21-25 | £14 6s |
| Housemaid | 21-25 | £16 2s |
| Nurse | 25-30 | £20 1s |
| Parlour maid | 25-30 | £20 6s |
| Laundry maid | 25-30 | £23 6s |
| Cook | 25-30 | £20 2s |
| Lady's maid | 30-35 | £24 7s |
| Cook-housekeeper | 40 | £20 2s |
| Housekeeper | 40 | £52 5s |

Coal was so crucial in Victorian times that Sunderland became a very important place.

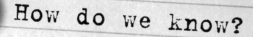

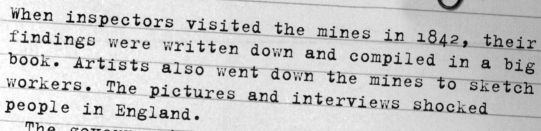

# How do we know?

When inspectors visited the mines in 1842, their findings were written down and compiled in a big book. Artists also went down the mines to sketch workers. The pictures and interviews shocked people in England.

The government brought in a new law which said that women, girls and young boys should not be allowed to work underground. Working hours were made shorter for other young workers and the mine owners were supposed to see that children went to school for a few hours a week.

We also have diaries, such as the one written by Mark Swaddle. Mark started work in 1867 and looked after the winding engine at Washington 'F' Pit. He wrote about the many accidents that took place in his pit and other local pits. After 'F' Pit was closed, the engine house was turned into a museum.

# At the Shipyard

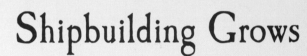

The year is 1876 and Alice's father is a foreman at one of the shipyards on the River Wear. He is talking to one of the workers. Meanwhile Alice's Uncle John is working as a carpenter, sawing wood to use inside the ship.

When Alice's uncle was young, all the ships were made from wood and worked by sails and wind power. The ship they are building now is an iron screw steamship or 'steamer'. This one will have sails as well so it can save on the cost of coal when it is windy.

Sunderland had some of the best shipyards in the world.

Crowds gathered to see the opening of the South Dock in 1850.

# Shipbuilding Grows

By 1815, Sunderland was the leading port for building wooden vessels that carried goods. In the 1830s a dock was built at Monkwearmouth by Sir Hedworth Williamson. This is now known as the North Dock. South Dock was built in 1850 and Hendon Dock followed in 1868.

During Victorian times the type of ships being built started to change. By the end of Queen Victoria's reign, most ships were made from iron and steel and worked by steam power rather than by sail. The last wooden ship to be built in Sunderland was finished in 1880, and the last sailing ship in 1893. Two famous sailing ships built in Sunderland were the *City of Adelaide* (1864) and the *Torrens* (1875). Shipbuilding involved many different jobs including riveting and boiler making.

...1840 SUNDERLAND IS THE BIGGEST SHIP-BUILDING TOWN IN THE WORLD...

# Other Kinds of Transport

A ship built in Sunderland

Railways began to transport people and goods from the 1820s onwards. In 1848 a grand station was opened at Monkwearmouth for people travelling to and from Gateshead and South Shields. This was the idea of George Hudson, who had also built South Dock and was known as 'The Railway King'. If passengers wanted to go south from Monkwearmouth, they had to walk across the bridge and catch a train from a different station.

As the seaside at Roker and Seaburn became popular, holidaymakers would travel to Monkwearmouth by train and then down to the beach by bus or tram. Sunderland saw its first trams in 1879. The trams were pulled by horses until 1900, when electric trams were introduced.

# A Sporting City

Sport became increasingly popular in Victorian times. Sunderland had a cricket team even before Victoria became queen, and its rugby club started in 1873. The football club was founded in 1879 and won the English Football League several times. There were also teams for hockey, bowls and tennis, as well as boat racing on the River Wear.

Sunderland Football Club was started by a group of young teachers! Does your teacher play football?

This is Sunderland Rugby Team in 1881. The photograph has been coloured by hand using paints. Notice the players' boots and the length of their shorts compared with ones worn today!

Now meet the ladies' tennis team from about 1900. Ladies enjoyed wearing these sports clothes because they were more comfortable than their usual everyday outfits and stiff underwear!

# Sunderland at War

Joan and Alan emerge from the air-raid shelter in their garden. They do not know what to say to each other. The houses around them have been badly damaged and the town is in ruins again.

During air raids in the past, Sunderland's railway station and Binn's – Joan's favourite shop for toys – had been destroyed. This time, the bombs seem to have hit more houses than ever before. Joan's dad says that the enemy bomb aimers in the planes can't have been very good if they were trying to hit the port and shipyards.

Joan and Alan both hope that their friends and neighbours all got to their shelters in time.

## Air Raids

Binns was destroyed during the Blitz in April 1941.

During World War Two, Sunderland was often the target for raids by enemy aircraft. They were aiming to hit Sunderland's shipyards. At sea, the Germans were sinking merchant ships to stop vital food and ammunition supplies getting to Britain. The shipyards were busy building new merchant ships to replace the ones that had been sunk. This made the shipyards an important target for German bombs.

Sadly the town centre and many homes were near to the river and shipyards and were damaged or destroyed in the bombing. Many people in the town were killed or injured because of the raids.

# Defending the Town

While soldiers were fighting overseas, there was another battle going on at home – on the Home Front. Big balloons called barrage balloons were put into the air to make it difficult for enemy aircraft to fly over the town. Anti-aircraft guns were placed in fields close to the edge of Sunderland and around the port. People volunteered to be special constables, firemen and air-raid wardens to help defend the town. Many children were evacuated from Sunderland during this time and sent to live in safer places.

Many women in Sunderland took over the men's jobs while they were away in the war.

Everyone in Britain was given a gas mask in case the Germans dropped gas bombs.

Sunderland has the second largest Remembrance Parade in the UK because so many men from the city were prisoners of war.

Today, people use poppies to remember people killed in the World Wars.

# Remembrance

Remembrance Day on 11th November is an important day all over the UK. This is the day when people remember the men and women who died fighting for the country in wars.

Sunderland has one of the biggest remembrance services and parades in the country. One reason for this is that many Sunderland men died or suffered as prisoners of war during World War Two. They were in the 125th Anti-Tank Regiment, which was captured by the enemy in Singapore in 1942. The men were held as prisoners for over three years and were treated badly. Life was made very difficult for them and 197 out of the 600 men never returned home. Survivors were released in August 1945, at the end of the war.

# A Famous Visitor

L. S. Lowry (1887–1976) was one of Britain's most famous painters. He lived in Lancashire but enjoyed visiting Sunderland. He often stayed at a particular hotel in Seaburn for weeks at a time.

Lowry is known for the distinctive way in which he painted people and animals. Many of his paintings and drawings can be seen at Sunderland Museum and Winter Gardens.

On the right is part of an imaginary diary from a schoolboy called Kevin in the 1960s. It is written at a time when old slums were being demolished in Sunderland.

Saturday was a weird day. I was going down to the sea front at Roker when I saw this old man sitting on a stool and drawing a picture. I like art so I got off my bike and asked him what he was doing. He said that he was trying to sketch the changes in Sunderland and might make the sketch into a painting when he went home.

As we were talking, a big metal ball swung into a nearby house and knocked it down! There were some boys and girls and a dog watching as this happened and the old man had drawn them in a very unusual way.

When I got home, my mum told me that the old man was a very famous painter called Mr Lowry and that he liked to come to Sunderland to watch the sea and make drawings. I wouldn't mind being an artist when I grow up.

Wow! I wish I could draw like that!

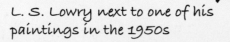
L. S. Lowry next to one of his paintings in the 1950s

TUDOR
1485-1603

STUART
1603-1714

GEORGIAN
1714-1837

VICTORIAN
1837-1901

MODERN
TIMES
1902-NOW

Many new houses were built in Sunderland in the 1950s and 1960s to replace the old slums.

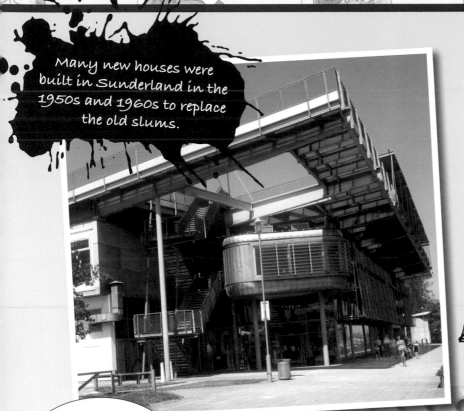

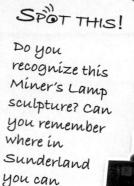

SP☍T THIS!

Do you recognize this Miner's Lamp sculpture? Can you remember where in Sunderland you can find it?

The National Glass Centre opened in 1998.

Sunderland's industries were changing in the 20th century.

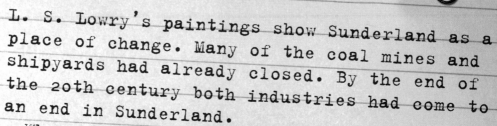

## How do we know?

L. S. Lowry's paintings show Sunderland as a place of change. Many of the coal mines and shipyards had already closed. By the end of the 20th century both industries had come to an end in Sunderland.

Where there was once a coal mine at Monkwearmouth, there is now a football ground – the Stadium of Light. Outside there is a huge copy of a miner's lamp to remind us what was once there. Where there were once shipyards, there is now a university and the National Glass Centre. The Glass Centre is here because Monkwearmouth was the first place in Britain to use stained glass.

Instead of building ships or mining coal, many workers in Sunderland today make cars.

27

# Sunderland Today and Tomorrow

Sunderland's history can be discovered and enjoyed in lots of ways. You can walk along the marina at North Dock, see interesting objects at Sunderland Museum and, at special times of the year, visit Washington 'F' Pit. The important thing to remember is that Sunderland's history is about the people who lived through difficult or exciting or dangerous times – people like Edwin, Anne and Kevin.

In 2010, Nissan announced that its new electric car would be built in Sunderland.

Sunderland Museum and Winter Gardens is at the heart of the city centre. You can see paintings by L. S. Lowry in the Art Gallery.

Sunderland Polytechnic became a university in 1992. Do you think people will always go to university? Could students learn at home instead, using webcams and the Internet to keep in touch with tutors?

The Stadium of Light opened in 1997. Seats at the stadium spell out the Sunderland phrase 'Ha'way the Lads'. Do you know what it means?

TUDOR
1485-1603

STUART
1603-1714

GEORGIAN
1714-1837

VICTORIAN
1837-1901

MODERN
TIMES
1902-NOW

This has been the home of Ashbrooke Sports Club since 1887. You will find it off West Lawn in the Ashbrooke area of the city.

Sunderland Pride is a special anchor that was built in Sunderland. It is outside the National Maritime Museum in London.

Monkwearmouth Station Museum has a Children's Gallery, especially for you!

You should feel proud to be a part of Sunderland's future.

## How will they know?

Will Sunderland always look like it does today? How will future generations know what Sunderland is like now? The Internet is a great way of recording what Sunderland is like. Photos, blogs and stories from tourists can all spread the word about our wonderful Sunderland. Or maybe you'll be famous one day and put Sunderland on the map!

# Glossary

**Abbey** – a building where monks or nuns live and work.

**AD** – a short way to write anno Domini, which is Latin and means 'in the year of Our Lord' or after the birth of Christ.

**Air raid** – an attack during World War Two when enemy planes dropped bombs on Britain. Sirens wailed to warn people the planes were coming, and people hid in air-raid shelters.

**Archaeologist** – a person who studies the past by examining buildings and objects left behind by previous people and cultures.

**Bait** – a word used in the north of England to mean food, especially a packed lunch. It can also mean any food used to attract fish or animals to a trap.

**Black Death, the** – another name for the Plague.

**Blitz** – when the Germans bombed towns during World War Two, it was called the Blitz.

**Catholic** – or Roman Catholic: a member of the Christian religion that considers the Pope its head.

**Cavalier** – a supporter of Charles I during the English Civil War. Also known as a Royalist.

**Charter** – written permission to do something. It is often a Royal Charter, meaning the king or queen has given permission.

**Cholera** – a deadly disease caused by filthy water.

**Christian** – one who believes Jesus Christ is the son of God and follows his teachings.

**Christianity** – the name of the religion whose followers believe Jesus Christ is the son of God.

**Civil war** – a war where people in the same country fight one another.

**Ferry** – a boat that takes people or things across water.

**Foreman/forewoman** – the man or woman in charge of workers.

**Gas mask** – a mask issued during World War Two to protect a person from breathing poisonous gas.

**Monastery** – a place where monks live and worship.

**Monk** – a male member of a religious community.

**Parliamentarian** – anyone who fought on the side of Parliament in the English Civil War.

**Pope** – the official name for the man who heads the Roman Catholic Church. The Pope lives in the Vatican in Rome.

**Port** – a place near to land where the water is deep enough for ships to stop and stay.

**Quarry** – a large place where people dig or blast stone out of the ground.

**Rector** – a person who is in charge of a set area (known as a parish) and everyone living in it who follows the Church of England religion, which has the king or queen as its head.

**Roundhead** – a nickname for a Parliamentarian in the English Civil War.

**Royalist** – anyone who fought on the side of King Charles I in the English Civil War.

**Trams** – a form of transport used before buses. They ran on rails dug into the streets and were attached to overhead electric cables, which gave them power. They could also be pulled by horses.

# Index

# Acknowledgements

The author and publishers would like to thank the following people for their generous help: Viv Anderson at Tyne and Wear Archives and Museums, Jennie Beale at Sunderland Museum, Ashbrooke Sports Club for allowing us to use images from their archives and City Library for their greatly appreciated co-operation.

The publishers would like to thank the following people and organizations
for their permission to reproduce material on the following pages:
p5: Fishbourne Museum, Chichester; p11: Craigy144/Wikipedia, Sunderland City Library; p13: ProhibitOnions/
Ian Dunster/Wikipedia, Gilbert Stuart/Wikipedia; p15: Sunderland City Library; p19: Discovery Museum and Sunderland Museum and Winter Gardens, courtesy of Tyne and Wear Archives and Museums; p21: www.nationalarchives.gov.uk;
p22: Sunderland Museum and Winter Gardens, courtesy of Tyne and Wear Archives and Museums; p23: Sunderland City Library, Ashbrooke Sports Club archives; p24: Sunderland City Library; p25: York Museums Trust (Castle Museum);
p26: Mary Evans Picture Library/IDA KAR; p28: The JPS/Wikipedia; p29: Ashbrooke Sports Club archives;
Green Lane/Wikipedia.

All other images copyright of Hometown World

Written by Keith Gregson
Educational consultant: Neil Thompson
Local history consultant: Martin Routledge
Designed by Sarah Allen

Illustrated by Kate Davies, Dynamo Limited, Virginia Gray,
Tim Hutchinson, John MacGregor, Leighton Noyes and Tim Sutcliffe
Additional photographs by Keith Gregson

First published by HOMETOWN WORLD in 2011
Hometown World Ltd
7 Northumberland Buildings
Bath BA1 2JB

www.hometownworld.co.uk

Copyright © Hometown World Ltd 2011

ISBN 978-1-84993-171-7

CELT
500 BC

ROMAN
AD 43-410

ANGLO-SAXON
AD 450-1066

VIKING
AD 865-1066

MEDIEVAL TIME
1066-1485